MW01241866

FOR OTHER BOOKS BY DARRELL SCOTT
GO TO:

www.dscottbooks.com

INDEX

INTRODUCTION

Prayer is fast becoming a lost art because of misunderstanding and misuse. Meditation and prayer are like two sides of the same coin, but they are not the same. Meditation is the forerunner to effective prayer. If one begins prayer without quieting his or her soul first, the prayer will be tainted with ego, and as a result, it becomes weakened, and usually impotent.

Meditation is also very much misunderstood. There are different forms and degrees of meditation. One of those is "reflective meditation" in which you focus your mind on one particular thing. For example, you can practice reflective meditation on a subject such as forgiveness or compassion. When something is reflective, it is bouncing off of something else, like a mirror.

Those who "walk in the spirit" have learned to embrace reflective meditation as a way of life. It is described in Psalm 1:

"Blessed is the man that walketh not in the counsel of the ungodly, nor standeth in the way of sinners, nor sitteth in the seat of the scornful. But his delight is in the law of the LORD; and in his law doth he meditate day and night. And he shall be like a tree planted by the rivers of water, that bringeth forth his fruit in his season; his leaf also shall not wither; and whatsoever he doeth shall prosper."

This reflective form of meditation is important because it keeps our mind focused on God's purpose for us instead of the focus being on our own thoughts. It also prevents us from "walking in the counsel of the ungodly". Reflective meditation is a key to acquiring wisdom.

However, there is another form that is very different from "reflective meditation", and that is "awareness meditation". Whereas reflective meditation focuses your thoughts, awareness meditation surrenders your thoughts, detaching from the white noise of frenzied thinking.

By "awareness" I mean consciousness without thinking. Living in the moment. I hear the bird singing without labeling the bird as a "sparrow" or "meadowlark". I see the beauty of the tree without labeling it as "oak" or "pine". I am alert and present, not lost in thought. This "awareness" is described in scripture as "being still". It is accepting the moment without analyzing it.

Awareness meditation is extremely important as a foundation for prayer because it disengages your mind and tunes into your spirit.

It is not thinking about something. It is, instead, completely disengaged from thought and enters the stillness of awareness, which is the "secret place of the Most High" described in Psalm 91.

It is also revealed in Psalm 23 where the Great Shepherd *"makes me to lie down in green pastures and leads me beside the still waters"*.

The emphasis in Psalm 23 is on rest (lie down) and stillness (still waters). Too many are wrestling in prayer before resting in Presence.

It is only after we lie down in green pastures and are led beside still waters that our soul is restored.

This is addressed in Isaiah 30:15 (NAS) where God says: *"In repentance and rest you will be saved. In quietness and trust is your strength, but you were not willing"*.

This is a powerful verse that has transformative wisdom for those with "ears to hear". It begins with repentance - - but repentance from what?

The word "repent" means more than just feeling sorry for something you did. It means to turn away from one thing toward another. There are 3 types of repentance mentioned in the Bible:

#1. Repentance from sin (Luke 24:47, Acts 2:38).

#2. Repentance from "dead works" (Hebrews 6:1).

#3. Repentance from noise and activity (Isaiah 30:15).

The third type of repentance: repentance from noise (especially mental noise) and activity is the least understood and the one most ignored.

Since repentance means to turn away from something toward something else, what are we repenting for in this

6

last verse? Since we are turning toward rest, quietness, and trust, the repentance must be a turning away from noise and activity.

It is this type of meditation that should precede prayer every time. A turning away, or repentance, from noise and activity, including the noise of our mind and thoughts. As we quiet the mind, we begin to engage the heart and true prayer can emerge untainted by self-interest and ego.

Awareness meditation and prayer work hand in hand to bring wholeness and fulfillment to our lives. However, they must be done right or they are a waste of time.

This book purposely focuses on prayer, but it is important to address awareness meditation as a forerunner to true prayer.

Awareness meditation is beginning to gain more traction around the world. It has been a practice of certain segments of our civilization for centuries. But while meditation is on the rise, prayer seems to be on the decline - - and I understand why. The misunderstanding and misuse of prayer is the key to its demise.

It is important to understand that prayer is not a means of getting God to do what you want him to do. Prayer is not a weapon to use against other people to get God to notice their faults so that they will change into the people you want them to be. Prayer is not a magical tool that changes all your outer circumstances.

True prayer brings you into harmony with the Source of all things: God. A communion that occurs deep within your spirit that allows incredible peace and joy to flow through you to others. It may or may not change the outer circumstances, but it allows peace in the middle of the storm. It allows joy to emerge from suffering and sorrow.

This book may offend good, well-meaning people who cannot receive anything other than the Bible. While I come from a Christian background, I will be referring to many sources of wisdom, both Biblical and otherwise.

"Wisdom cries aloud. She utters her voice in the streets" (Prov. 1:20). These were the words penned by a wise and mighty king many centuries ago. Solomon was pointing out that wisdom is continually speaking in every place if we simply have the ears to hear her voice.

"Wisdom cries out in the streets". I think that this is God's way of saying that wisdom is not limited to any one source - - - including the Bible! Paul instructed us to learn from nature (II Corinthians 11:14) - - and from poets (Acts 17:28). The Psalmist (Psalm 8:3) instructed us to observe the stars and constellations to learn truth; and Job was instructed by God (Job 39) to learn from observing the animal kingdom.

Wisdom is available through poems, songs, movies, plays, books, and everyone and everything around us! Therefore, you will not only see Bible scripture quoted in this book, but you will also hear wisdom from many people coming from different cultures, backgrounds,

8

and belief systems. Truth is truth even when uttered by sources that you may or may not consider to be tainted.

TO BE – OR NOT TO BE
darrell scott

So many seek and cannot find
The Source of life they call "divine"
An essence so elusive sought in vain

For what they fail to comprehend
Is that the answer lies within
They have what they are trying to obtain

They pray, and chant, and meditate
And hope that they can find their fate
They're like a wave that's searching for the sea

While deep within lies all they need
Just waiting like a pregnant seed
The choice is theirs: To be or not to be!

Chapter 1
PRAYER VS. MEDITATION

Prayer was never intended to be a self-serving communication tool to get what we want. Too often, prayer is viewed as a magical formula, like rubbing the bottle and hoping a genie appears to grant our wishes.

People will pray for a new car, a new home, a raise at work, or even to win the lottery. Sometimes that prayer is incorporated with a bribe, like, "God, if you will let me win the $40,000,000 lottery, I will give half of it to the poor and homeless." However, you can't trick the Creator by hiding greed beneath the façade of charitable generosity.

Too often prayer is ignored until a crisis arises. When a friend or family member gets sick, prayer is brought out of the closet to ask for their health or healing. This is far less selfish than asking to win the lottery, but it is still a very limited form of prayer, though a valid and understandable one. It boils down to a one way communication consisting of a request for relief.

True prayer, as pointed out by Richard Rohr, requires us to take off our *calculating mind* and put on our *contemplative mind*. The calculating mind operates from the soul (psyche) and is self-centered. The contemplative mind operates from the spirit (pnuema) and is Source, or God-centered.

One of the vastly overlooked truths from scripture is the understanding of the separation of soul and spirit:

"For the word of God is living and active. Sharper than any double-edged sword, it penetrates even to dividing of soul and spirit" (Hebrews 4: 12 NIV).

The Bible teaches that we are transformed by the renewing of our minds (Rom. 12:2). It encourages us to let the same mind which was in Christ, be in us (Phil. 2:5). To be fleshly minded is death, but to be spiritually minded is life and peace (Rom 8:6).

The Divine Source of all of creation is not merely a vending machine whose sole function is to provide gifts whenever we plead for them. Mother Teresa said, *"Prayer is not asking. Prayer is putting oneself in the hands of God, at His disposition, and listening to His voice in the depth of our hearts."*

When "asking for things" is the essence of one's prayer, it reveals a level of spiritual immaturity. Contrast the request to win the lottery with the prayer of Francis of Assisi:

"Lord, make me an instrument of your peace.
Where there is hatred, let me sow love,
Where there is injury, pardon
Where there is doubt, faith,
Where there is despair, hope,
Where there is darkness, light,
Where there is sadness, joy.
O Divine Master, grant that I may not so much
seek to be consoled as to console,
Not so much to be understood as to understand,
Not so much to be loved, as to love;

11

For it is in giving that we receive,
It is in pardoning that we are pardoned,
It is in dying that we awake to eternal life."

What about the Hindu prayer from the Atharva Veda:

"Supreme Lord, let there be peace in the sky
and in the atmosphere;
Let there be peace in the plant world
and in the forests;
Let the cosmic powers be peaceful;
Let the Brahman, the true essence
and source of life, be peaceful;
Let there be undiluted and fulfilling
peace everywhere."

Listen to this prayer of the Native Americans:

"O Great Spirit of our Ancestors,
I raise my pipe to you.
To your messengers the four winds,
And to Mother Earth who provides for your children.
Give us the wisdom to teach our children
to love, to respect,
And to be kind to each other s
o that they may grow
with peace in mind.
Let us learn to share all the good things
you provide for us on this Earth."

Finally, consider a prayer, written as a song, by Keith Green, who died at the young age of 28 in a plane crash. Keith personally provided seven houses for people in need, from homeless folks to single moms, at his own expense. Listen to the start of his melodic prayer:

"Oh Lord, you're beautiful, Your face is all I see,
For when your eyes are on this child, Your grace
abounds in me".

The prayers of the mature only ask to be instruments and channels of grace to others. They ask not for themselves, except for enlightenment and the ability to spread light where there is darkness.

Mahatma Ghandi said, *"Prayer is not asking. It is a longing of the soul. It is daily admission of one's weakness. It is better in prayer to have a heart without words than words without a heart."*

So, if prayer is not asking, what is it?

Take a closer look at the most quoted and well-known prayer of all: In Christian tradition it is called "The Lord's Prayer". It is short and simple, but full of content.

Jesus gave it to his disciples after they said to him, "Lord teach us to pray" (Luke 11:1). The instructions that he gave them, following that request, were not meant to be repeated as a mantra, but instead, to be a pattern for our interaction and communication with and from the Source of all life.

Before looking at this great prayer, it is important to see the connection between meditation and prayer. The pattern given by Jesus goes like this: First quiet meditation, followed by Source centered, spiritual prayer. Christians often practice prayer without meditation, and Buddhists practice meditation without prayer. However, meditation and prayer were meant to work together.

Jesus was often known to slip away to "lonely" or "solitary" places to pray (Luke 5:16, Mark 1:35). Solitary places lend themselves to contemplative meditation. H.G. Salter wrote, "*Meditation before prayer matures our concepts - - and meditation is like the tuning of an instrument, and setting it for the harmony of prayer. The great reason that our prayers are ineffective is that we do not meditate before them.*"

Mother Teresa once said, "*The fruit of silence is prayer*". She was saying that out of silence comes fruit, and that fruit is prayer. We pray from the inside out, as Jesus put it, "*Out of your innermost being shall flow rivers of living water*". But it begins with a quieting of the chattering mind; a settling of the soul; enabling us to hear the "still small voice" that speaks from our spirit.

In both Christianity and Judaism, the scriptural admonition was to "*Be still and know that I am God*". Both Quakers and Native Americans practiced silence before prayer.

An author by the name of Adyashanti (a name that means "primordial peace") wrote a book called *True Meditation*. In it he points out that true meditation is simple and does not require years of practice.

14

It is not a practice of technique and discipline but a letting go of both. It is allowing the mind to settle down and tapping into the peace that lies beneath the realm of soul in the realm of spirit.

It is not the mind's attempt to acquire peace - - - it is quieting the mind and allowing the spirit's release of peace from within. I want to repeat that phrase: Meditation is not the mind's attempt to acquire peace - - - it is the spirit's release of peace from within, through a quieted mind.

Attempts to "find peace" always end in futility because peace is not lost. It does not need to be found. It resides within your spirit, waiting to be released. The pursuit of peace in the outer, physical, material world is doomed to failure from the start.

In the book of Psalms it says, *"He who dwelleth in the secret place of the Most High shall abide under the shadow of the Almighty"* (Psalm 91:1). Scripture, sages, poets, and philosophers all agree that peace is not to be pursued, but to be released from within.

Several years ago this great statement from Psalms inspired me to write the following poem.

In the Quiet
darrell scott

In the quiet, I find peace,
Where the outside noises cease

When my mind has settled down
And my thoughts no longer race
In the chambers of my spirit
I have found a secret place

There the unseen things embrace us
The invisible that's real
And we there enjoy the treasure
That activity would steal

Hear the whisper of the poets
As they beckon us to know
Of that inner sanctuary
Where we seldom ever go

In the quiet of my being
Creativity is born
And it rises to the surface
To a world that's hurt and torn

Deep within me love replaces
All the anger and the fear
In the stillness is a knowing
Who I AM and why I'm here

(Use QR Code to see video of this poem)

16

Chapter 2
PROMINENCE
"Our Father"

The great prayer, taught by Jesus to his disciples, consists of 12 sections with acknowledgements of Prominence, Place, Praise, Participation, Provision, Pardon, Prevention, Protection, Possession, Power, Presence, and Permanence. Let's explore these a little deeper.

Here is a quick overview of these 12 "P's" found in the model prayer given by Jesus and found in Matthew 6 (KJV) :

Prominence:	"Our Father"
Place:	"Which art in heaven"
Praise:	"Hallowed be thy name"
Participation:	"Thy kingdom come. Thy will be done on earth, as it is in heaven."
Provision:	"Give us this day our daily bread"
Pardon:	"And forgive us our debts, as we forgive our debtors"
Prevention:	"And lead us not into temptation"
Protection:	"But deliver us from evil"
Possession:	"For thine is the kingdom - -"
Power:	"- - and the power - -"
Presence:	"- - and the glory"
Permanence:	"Forever. Amen"

The "Great Prayer" begins with an acknowledgement of the prominence of the Divine - - - "Our Father". This is a contemplative, meditative prelude to the rest of the prayer.

The Source of all things is referred to through many descriptive words. In this prayer, it is "Father". There are so many implications to the word "father".

Some people have had negative experiences with their earthly fathers and the term itself can carry bad images. But in this prayer, "Father" is the loving originator and provider of life itself, the Source of all things.

The title is not as important as what the title represents. For example, Native Americans referred often to "The Great Spirit".

In the Christian Bible, God is referred to in many metaphorical terms: The Father of Lights, the King of the Ages, The Almighty, Alpha and Omega, and many more. As Juliet said to Romeo, *"What's in a name? That which we call a rose, by any other name would smell as sweet."*

The Lord's Prayer begins by an acknowledgment of the invisible "Father" or first Source of everything. Note that it is "our" Father, not someone else's. And it is not just "my" Father. It is "our Father, both individually and collectively.

Each one of us is connected and has access to the prominent Origin of all creation. It is hidden within us, wanting to be revealed through us to all of us. In this Source we live, and breathe, and have our being (Acts

17:28). It is revealed through reverent stillness. It speaks to us in a "still small voice".

The Jewish scriptures give us clear instruction to *"Be still, and know that I AM God"*.

True prayer begins with an acknowledgement of the prominence of the invisible over the visible; of energy over matter, of source over expression, of the spiritual over the natural.

For example, let's look at electricity versus a light bulb. The light bulb may seem more real because you can see it, hold it in your hand, break it, etc. However, the light bulb is useless unless it is plugged into the source, which is - - - electricity.

You can see the light bulb but you cannot see the electricity. The light bulb simply manifests electricity in the form of light when plugged into the source.

Which is more powerful or prominent: the light bulb or electricity? Everyone would agree that electricity is the powerful and prominent source, while the light bulb is the conduit for the manifestation of the source.

Too many people are like light bulbs who have failed to plug into the Source. They believe that the only reality is what they can see, taste, smell, feel, and hear. They live, as Henry Thoreau wrote, "Lives of quiet desperation". Why? Because they have failed to acknowledge the invisible Source that is available to them. They choose the prominence of self over Source.

Look at the four prayers I mentioned earlier by Francis of Assisi, Hindus, Native Americans, and Keith Green. All of these prayers start with the words "Lord", "Supreme Lord", "Oh Great Spirit, and "Oh Lord". Each acknowledges the prominence of the Divine.

You will find this to be true in the famous prayers of every faith, whether Christian, Hindu, Jewish, Muslim, or Native American. They all begin with an acknowledgement of the prominence of the invisible Source. Immature prayers seldom begin by honoring God. Too often they begin with requests and reminders of our personal needs.

If our focus is on our needs instead of the Source of our provision we will resort to fruitless, desperate, hope instead of confident faith. What we focus on we express or manifest. A focus on our problem will never bring a solution.

Albert Einstein once said, "You can never solve a problem on the level on which it was created." A focus on poverty will never bring wealth. A focus on misery will never bring joy. Prayer is the communication stream, whether vocal or silent, that gives access to the answers within our spirit to every problem and need we may encounter.

Wayne Dyer wrote a book titled, _There is a Spiritual Solution to Every Problem_. I recommend that you read that book to fully understand that Our Father has already provided answers to any question or problem that we could ask or encounter.

Prayer is not necessarily talking out loud to an invisible being that you hope is out there somewhere listening. It is a confident communication between your spirit and the "Great Spirit" referred to here as "our Father". As you come into reverent alignment, you have access to all that God is and all that he provides.

You have the physical DNA of your natural father, but you also have the spiritual DNA of your spiritual father. By acknowledging that you are not the Source, but the participator with that Source, you bring yourself into alignment with the Creator of all things.

The same man (Jesus) who said "*I can of mine own self do nothing*", also said "*All things that the Father has are mine*". Is this a contradiction? No! It reveals a truth that few come to understand.

Your false self, your ego, which is created by your human thought, cannot accomplish anything of lasting value. Your true self, your spirit, already has everything that you will ever need through connection to the Source. If you have an ear to hear, that rings true. If not, it will sound like ethereal mumbo jumbo.

There was a time in my life, before I traded religion for spirituality, when I prayed the same way I thought. A continuous stream of words came out of my mouth as I would plead with, instruct, and admonish God with my needs, my thoughts, and my opinions.

What I thought was prayer was nothing more than the

white noise of my mind spilling out into words. I was a light bulb that had not yet encountered electricity.

EGO'S SCAM
darrell scott

Believing that my thoughts are me
Has caused me such confusion
Creating false identity
Resulting in illusion

My prayers were needy, desperate cries
I asked and begged and pleaded
A verbal list of my desires
The things I thought I needed

But yielding to a quiet mind
Exposing ego's scam
By letting go, I've come to know
In stillness - - who I AM

It is also important to understand that "our Father" is not a domineering male figure. First of all, God is a spirit, not a material flesh and blood being like us. A spirit does not have male or female organs and is gender neutral. However, there are characteristics of both male and female qualities in God, since he made both male and female in his image (Gen. 1:27).

Among the many names attributed to God is the Old Testament, Jewish name of El Shaddai. Shad means "breast" in the Hebrew language. Shaddai means "double-breasted".

When this name is used it reflects the feminine side of God. The Holy Spirit is compared to a dove, which has the gentle qualities of the feminine.

God comforts us like a mother comforts her child (Isa. 66:13). God is like a mother eagle hovering over her young (Deut. 32:11). Like a woman who would never forget her nursing child, God will not forget us (Isa. 49:15). There are many other verses in the Bible that show the feminine side of God's spirit.

So, I hope you are not encumbered with the image of God being an old, bearded man, sitting on a throne somewhere in outer space. If you can realize that "Our Father" is an acknowledgment of the Source of all life, the fountain of living water that Jesus referred to when he said, *"Out of your innermost being will flow rivers of living water"*.

It is not a Source "out there" somewhere. It is a Source that abides within us and is accessible when we become "aware".

As long as we live life as an unplugged light bulb, we will never know the peace and joy that is ours by simply acknowledging the invisible Source of power, and plugging into that Source.

Behind every manifestation; behind all "matter"; behind *EVERTHING*: is Source! When we recognize the prominence of the Source over the "self", we have entered the spirit of prayer.

FORM & FORMLESS
darrell scott

A beautiful mansion of classic design
A structure that all could admire
"But where did it come from?" I thought to myself
And so I set out to inquire

The homeowner told me the house started out
As blueprints designed by a friend
An architect labored to lay out a plan
Expressed by his paper and pen

I asked where the blueprints and plan had come from
He smiled and replied, "From my head.
My thoughts turned to paper, then blueprints, and then
The house was completed" he said.

So what birthed the thoughts that expressed as a house?
The questions went deeper, of course
The thoughts came from somewhere and as I pressed on
I entered the ultimate Source!

Exploring the place where the wonder set in
A place only spirit can see
A place that transcended the visible realm
Where substance and form cease to be

The mansion, the blueprints, the plan, and the thoughts
Were all different forms of expression
Emerging from formless, invisible Source
That ultimate place of perfection

Chapter 3
PLACE
"Which art in heaven"

Now we move on to the second part of this first segment: *"which art in heaven"*. The term, 'in heaven", implies much more than an image of clouds, planets, or galaxies. It should be understood as the invisible, spiritual realm. Our "Father" (source), which art in "heaven" (the spiritual, invisible realm).

The spiritual realm of heaven is not somewhere out there beyond the galaxies. It is a dimension found within us. Jesus admonished his followers not to seek the Kingdom "here or there", referring to any material temple or place. Instead he proclaimed, *"The kingdom of God is within you"*. Buddhism teaches the same thing: *"Peace comes from within. Do not seek it without"*.

Robert Browning, the renowned English poet, in his poem, *From Paracelsus*, wrote: "

"Truth is within ourselves. There is an inmost center in us all, where truth abides in fullness; and to know - - rather consists in opening out a way whence the imprisoned splendor may escape than in effecting entry for a light supposed to be without".

Wow! That poem describes the difference between religion and spirituality!

Paul wrote about an experience (II Corinthians 12:2) that he had where he was "caught up" to the third heaven. He did not know whether he was in the body or out of the body. Interesting!

He also experienced things that he said could not be "uttered" or explained. He was in a realm of peace that "passes understanding" and a place of "joy unspeakable and full of glory" - - the third heaven. But where is this "third heaven"?

Some believe that the first heaven is the physical realm within earth's gravitational pull. The second heaven is everything in the universe beyond, including the planets, galaxies, etc. However the third heaven is a realm that supersedes the physical. It is the spiritual realm.

The human body, soul, and spirit could be compared to the first, second, and third heavens. The existence of the human body is never questioned because it is so obvious. It is a physical object that interacts with a physical world through the 5 senses.

The body has been studied, explored, and dissected for thousands of years by science and medicine. We know everything there is to know about the 700 muscles, the 4,000 tendons, the 360 joints, 206 bones in an average adult.

While it does not take faith to believe that the human body exists, it does take faith in the scientific and medical experts to know these facts because most of us have never taken the time to count them!

But when it comes to soul and spirit, we have no tangible "body" to dissect and examine. We know that such things as joy, peace, anger, depression, love, hate, and contentment exist, but no one has ever actually seen those things. We have seen the expression and result, but never the things themselves, because they are invisible.

The soul (*Greek word: psyche*) has been studied and written about by many psychologists and psychiatrists who have divided it into several compartments such as Freud's id, ego, and super ego, which are merely terms to describe what he believed to be different aspects of the psyche.

We know far less about the soul than we do the body. In fact, psychology is a fairly new field of study, beginning in 1879, while the study of the human body dates back to 1600 B.C.

But the study of the human spirit, compared to the study of the body or soul, is still in its infancy. Religious leaders, mystics, poets and philosophers have been the primary explorers in this arena.

Because the spirit is even harder to define than the soul, there have been many erroneous teachings and weird applications in this realm. That which is psychic, or soulish, can appear spiritual and the undiscerning can easily be deceived into thinking that one is the other.

The Christian Bible speaks of a clear difference between the soul (psyche) and spirit (pnuema), even stating that they can be *"divided asunder"* or separated.

Watchman Nee, a great Chinese mystic and writer defined soul as intellect, emotions, and volition, or will. He then defined spirit as: intuition, conscience, and communion, or connectedness with Source.

While the soul is in close connection with the material, emotional, and intellectual world, the spirit remains detached from all that is external and connects with the Source of universal wisdom and with the spirits of others.

Both are connected, but to different spheres. However, they are connected to each other very closely, in fact, so closely that they are hard to tell apart at times.

N. Michael Murphy wrote that the soul craves connectedness with our world while the spirit teaches detachment from earthly concerns.

This causes inner conflict if we fail to understand the differences and functions of each. Many people spend their entire life trying to figure out who they really are because of this conflict.

The soul tends to be judgmental, constantly comparing, dissecting, and defining while the spirit is geared to discern. The opinion of the soul can be misunderstood as an intuitive knowing in the spirit. Sympathy felt in the soul can be confused with compassion in the spirit.

SOUL AND SPIRIT
darrell scott

Soul and spirit aren't the same
(as so many do proclaim)
Though they both remain invisible
The two are not the same

One is Source and one expression
One the thinker, one the thought
One eternal, one but fleeting
One the teacher, one the taught

Mind, emotions, and volition
All components of the soul
Meant as servants to the spirit
As they each express their role

While the spirit's intuition
And communion with the Source
Has a conscience there to guide it
As it navigates its course

Soul and spirit, separated
Meant to work in harmony
Bringing peace and joy and presence
To a life that's been set free

With the power of a lion
And the meekness of a lamb
Be aware, in quiet stillness
Of the present, great, I AM

Psychology is the study of the soul, and comes from the Greek word "psyche". But little is said about the need for pneumatology which is the study of the human spirit, from the Greek word "pneuma". Study of the soul without understanding the deeper realm of spirit can lead us down endless rabbit trails.

The body is like the house, while the soul is the living room within the house, and the spirit is the closet in the living room.

Listen to the words of Jesus: *"But thou, when thou prayest, enter into thy closet, and when thou hast shut thy door, pray to thy Father which is in secret; and thy Father which seeth in secret shall reward thee openly."*
(Matthew 6:6 KJV)

This "prayer closet" is not a physical room in your house - - it is the inner sanctuary of your spirit. Go into your spirit and shut the door to all outside distraction. Still your mind and soul, and commune in the spirit.

Notice that it says, *"pray to thy Father, which is in secret"*. The closet *is* the "secret place of the Most High". As we pray, or commune, within our spirit, the reward, or manifestation, will emerge, and be expressed openly. It starts on the inside and works out.

So, when we address the phrase, "Our Father, which art in Heaven" we need to understand what and where "heaven" is. It is true that the Source is everywhere and in everything, but the intimate relationship can only be experienced in the Holy of Holies.

30

It is in the "secret place of the Almighty" that we find total peace and unspeakable joy. And that place is the spirit within us.

The first of the 10 sections of the Lord's Prayer is an acknowledgement of the prominence of the Divine. It is acknowledging the Divine within you, not out there in the ether. It requires humility to recognize that your ego, or false self, is not in control, but it is "Our Father, which art in heaven". It is the Divine within you and I.

Approaching prayer with a reverence for the Divine requires quieting the mind, and yielding to the inner Source. *"Be still - - and know that I AM God"*.

This may be a verbal or a silent acknowledgement. The spiritually mature learn to live in prayer - - to pray without ceasing. They live in constant, reverent awareness of the Spirit within. When you fully acknowledge the prominence of Spirit, you will find no need to ask for things. You will realize that all things are yours and requests are replaced with gratitude.

In these words, "Our Father, which art in heaven", is a recognition of sovereignty, majesty, and grace. Your prayers will be more effective when they begin with an acknowledgement of the prominence of God's spirit within you.

Your spirit is *"the candle of the Lord"* and when acknowledged will become a flame! Savor the essence of that phrase "Our Father, which art in heaven" and it will lead you to the next section of the prayer.

Chapter 4
PRAISE
"Hallowed be thy name"

Nancy asked her son Jimmy what he had learned in a recent church service. Jimmy said, "We learned that God's name is Harold." "You learned what?" his mom exclaimed. "We learned that God's name is Harold - - You know, in the Lord's Prayer it says, 'Our Father, which art in heaven, Harold be thy name!" answered Jimmy.

Of course, we know that Jimmy heard the word "hallowed" and assumed it was "Harold", the name of God, as in "Harold be thy name".

While there are many attempts to name or define God, none are sufficient. In Jewish tradition, originally, the name of God was too sacred to pronounce. It was simply written in four consonants: YHWH, and was unspeakable. Over time, attempts were made to "name" the Divine and 3 primary names emerged: Yaweh, Adonai, and Elohim.

Soon there were dozens of names for the Jewish Divinity, each describing a different aspect of God. Names like Elyon, El Olam, Yaweh-Jireh, Yaweh-Rapha,, Yaweh Nissi, etc. One of the many Jewish names was El Shaddai, which means "the breasted one" and acknowledges the feminine qualities of the Divine. But, as with anything, the more it is dissected and defined, the less we see the true essence of the whole. We lose sight of Source and only view manifestation.

In the first verse of the Tao Te Ching, Lao-tzu writes, *"The Tao that can be told is not the eternal Tao. The name that can be named, is not the eternal name. The Tao is both named and nameless. As nameless, it is the origin of all things. As named, it is the Mother of 10,000 things. Ever desireless, one can see the mystery. Ever desiring, one only sees the manifestations. And the mystery itself is the doorway to all understanding."*

This passage is pregnant with revelation and I will only attempt to scratch the surface of its meaning. "Tao" means "Way". Here, Lao-tzu tells us that the minute we name something as "The Way" it cannot be "The Way", because in defining it we limit it. God cannot be limited to words. The Source of our being is not Christian or Muslim or Jewish, or Hindu, or Buddhist.

Lao-tzu also says that "The Way" is both named and nameless. As *nameless* it is the origin of all things - - it is the Source, or God. However, naming it or labeling it moves it from the indefinable, unlimited realm to the realm of "matter" or "things". So when "The Way" is *named*, it becomes the "Mother of 10,000 things". The unnamed is "Father" or origin. The named is "Mother" in manifestation or expression.

Science would view it this way: "Father" is energy, while "Mother" is matter. One is source and one is expression. In an earlier chapter, we saw the difference between electricity and a light bulb. Electricity is the unseen source that cause the light bulb, the visible manifestation, to light up a room.

33

The light bulb without electricity would be a useless piece of equipment with no ability to function. The electricity without a means of expression would be power without manifestation.

So, in the Lord's Prayer, there is no name given, simply a reverence for the "un-named" name. Why is this important? Because it prevents us from "defining" God. It leaves room for awe-inspiring praise and worship of the Source of everything. "Our Father, which art in heaven. Hallowed be thy name."

To "hallow" is to respect. Praise requires awareness and appreciation. Being aware and appreciative of the Source within us results in praise. Praise is expressed in many ways. There is exuberant expressions of praise, there is a softer, verbal appreciative praise, and then there is a deep, silent acknowledgement of gratitude.

Lao-tzu also says, *"Ever desireless, one can see the mystery. Ever desiring, one can only see the manifestations."* This is a profound truth that escapes the understanding of many.

In essence, he says that when we "empty ourselves of desire", the blinders fall from our spiritual eyes and we are able to see the mystery. He goes on to say that the mystery is the doorway to all understanding.

If we "desire" we do not see the mystery, only the manifestations, and therefore cannot pass through the doorway of all understanding. This is why the "asking" mode of prayer is immature and very limiting.

We only see what we desire instead of "*seeing Him who is invisible*".

It also reveals that we have not become aware of all the answers provided by the Source which has been hidden within our human spirit. We are still seeking joy, peace, and wholeness through "things" that we desire.

The 23rd Psalm is the most well-known of all the Psalms. It is often quoted at funerals, but this beautiful discourse was not intended as a farewell to the dead, but as a roadmap for the living. Notice that it begins with the statement, "The Lord is my Shepherd, I shall not want".

This psalm begins at a level of maturity that few experience. "I shall not want". This matches perfectly with the first verse of the Tao which teaches us that: "Ever desireless, one sees the mystery - - ever desiring, one only sees the manifestation!"

There is an interesting passage in scripture that points out that Moses knew God's *ways* while Israel was focused on God's *works*. Many people today are focused on the works of God, while a few are focused on his ways.

Those who focus on his *works* will never fully experience the fulfillment of "knowing God". They will only know the manifestation of his power.

Those who focus on his *ways* will come to know his as the Source, and will come to understand the mystery.

THE HIDDEN
darrell scott

Much doctrine and teaching has hidden Your presence
Religion and dogma, distorting Your essence
You're sought by so many, and found by so few
You're easy to find, if the seekers just knew

They go to a building with singing and prayer
They reach out to touch You and hope You are there
They visit Your presence but fail to abide
They don't understand that You're always inside

They claim that they'll find You, whatever the cost
But they don't understand that You never were lost
Stop searching "out there", it's like chasing the wind
For That which you seek for is hidden within!

An acknowledgment of prominence (*Our Father*) and an understanding of place (which art in heaven), leads to praise (*Hallowed be thy name*).

When we empty ourselves in humility and acknowledge the prominence of the Source, and when we realize that the place where that Source abides is within us, it leads us to an attitude of praise. This opens the door to the fourth section, which is participation.

Chapter 5
PARTICIPATION
"Thy kingdom come, thy will be done
on earth as it is in heaven"

The great misunderstanding of this phrase in the Lord's prayer, is that somehow a kingdom that exists on there in heaven somewhere, needs to descend onto the earth. The kingdom does come - - but not down from the sky. It comes from out of you and I.

The location of the kingdom was given to us by Jesus himself. He said, *"The kingdom of God is within you"*. He also said that it would not come with outward observation.

The parables of the leaven and the mustard seed show us that the emergence of the kingdom takes place within our spirit and slowly emerges to impact the world around us.

So the kingdom of God resides within our spirit and comes out of us like rivers of living water. God has implanted his incorruptible seed in the form of powerful promises within us, so that we can partake of his own divine nature.

There is an interesting passage in the Christian Bible found in II Peter 1:3-4:

"His divine power has given us everything we need for a godly life through our knowledge of him who called us by his own glory and goodness. Through these he has

given us his very great and precious promises, so that through them you may participate in the divine nature, having escaped the corruption in the world caused by evil desires."

The words above are pregnant with meaning. They contain the key to living a life of purpose and fulfillment. So let's break these 2 verses down in bite-size bits to help us understand them better.

First of all, this passage informs of us of the ability to participate in the divine nature! This sounds like heresy to the religious mind. But participation is conditional. It requires an acknowledgement of God's prominence - - His divine power.

It also acknowledges that we have (past tense) been given everything we need for a complete life. *Everything*! When we fully understand that, we cease asking and start praising! Read the first chapter of Ephesians where Paul says that His divine power has given us everything we need - - but it is accessed *"through our knowledge of him"*.

So how do we obtain the *"knowledge of him"*? He told us the answer to that in Psalm 46:10, *"Be still, and know that I am God"*. It is only when we choose to detach from the constant stream of thoughts, racing through our mind, that we can ever realize what we already know.

Revelation is not information that comes to our brain through teaching. It is awareness of what we already know - - revealed from our spirit when we stop the noisy clamoring of our thought life!

Let me repeat that in another way. Revelation is when we become aware in our mind of what our spirit already knows. All of us have experienced times when we heard something that we had never heard before, and instantly knew that it was true.

In I Corinthians 12:8 this is called "*the word of knowledge*", and is one of the gifts of the Spirit. It is the intuitive element of the spirit in operation.

Observation of, or stimulation from, an outside source may trigger it, but the knowledge was already there. This is why it is so important to visit the inner sanctuary of our spirit, in order to access the knowledge of God, that has always been there.

The "*participation in the divine nature*" is given to us through the "very great and precious promises". Reread II Peter 1:3-4 very carefully. The words are pregnant with meaning and promise you everything you could ever hope for in life - - if you are willing to hear and obey what it says.

It is promising you that you can participate in the divine nature of God! Not just as a separate creature, at arms length away, but you can realize your oneness with God.

You can live and move in, and be a part of the creative force of the universe!

However, the first step is an acknowledgement that the Source has *already* given you everything you will ever need. You may not feel like it, and there may be no empirical, physical evidence that it is true to your senses, but it has already been fully accomplished within your human spirit.

Remember the previous advice to *"Be still, and know that I AM God"*? It requires spending time in the stillness to realize that *"all things are yours"* (I Cor. 3:21). Our entire perspective changes when we recognize what is true, rather than what we think, or feel, is true.

Also notice that this participation comes when we have *"escaped the corruption in the world caused by evil desires"*. This lines up with the first verse of the Tao which says, *"Ever desireless, one can see the mystery"*.

Notice that in the previous verse, Peter says: *"having escaped the corruption in the world caused by evil desires"*.

He is saying that the corruption is caused by evil desires. All wars, slavery, poverty, hunger, prejudice, and entitlement are the results of evil desires. Greed that believes that the answer lies in owning more, dominating others, and winning at any cost.

When we quiet our mind and tap into the inner kingdom with a sacred reverence, we begin to participate in the divine nature.

Eckhart Tolle said, *"To be in the consciousness of the "now" moment and to practice awareness of the divine Presence is what Jesus means in his Sermon on the Mount when he says, 'Take no thought for your life.' From this state of Being comes great creativity - - Instead of constantly thinking, we become still and quiet, and we become conscious of being conscious. This is the realization of I AM, the realization of Being, our essence identity.*

When we are rooted in that, thinking becomes the servant of awareness, rather than a self-serving (ego) activity. It becomes creative, empowered."

If the kingdom is within us, as Jesus said it was, then that is the starting point. For God's kingdom to come and his will to done on earth as it is in heaven, it begins within us and is manifested in the world around us. We are in the physical world, but not of it. Our participation is required for the kingdom to move from the invisible realm to the visible.

It is important to understand, however, that just because the promises have been given to us does not mean that automatically become participators in the divine nature. It requires us acknowledging the kingdom within, and expressing it without.

"For as many as are the promises of God, in Him they are 'Yes'; therefore also through Him is our 'Amen' to the glory of God through us." (II Corinthians 1:20 NAS)

So, the promises are *"yes"* - - - but they find their

41

fulfillment when they become an "*amen*" through us! This happens when we choose to participate in the divine nature through refusing to identify with our thoughts. By observing and detaching from them, we develop an ear to hear the still small voice of the spirit.

It is that still small voice, the Word of God, that divides our soul and spirit, enabling us to partake of the divine nature through the promises that He has given.

As we abide in the Source, the seeds of promise become the fruit of the spirit. The "yes" becomes an "amen"!

Christians recognize that Jesus was the manifestation of the glory of God, and was one with the Father. They acknowledge him as the "light of the world", the "miracle worker", the "Son of God".

However, it is rare to find a Christian who sees themselves as a "manifestation of the glory of God" or as "one with God", or the "light of the world" or the "miracle worker, or "a son of God".

And yet, Jesus said that we have been given the glory of God. He prayed that we would be one with the Father even as (in the same way) that he was one with the Father. (John 17:22)

He said that "*You are the light of the world*" (Matthew 5:14) He said that we would do greater works than he did (John 14:12). And John wrote, "*But as many as received him, to them gave he power to become the sons of God - -*" (John 1:12).

We squander our spiritual inheritance when we refuse to acknowledge and participate in the divine nature, through the promises that are planted as seeds in our human spirit.

So as we pray the Lord's Prayer, we move from acknowledging the **prominence** of Source, that resides, (**place**), within us, to **praising** (or hallowing) the name that cannot be named, to **participation** in the divine nature by releasing the inner kingdom into outer manifestation.

A modified version of the "Lord's Prayer" up to this point, might sound like this: *"Our Source that resides within us, we stand in awe and praise of your unlimited power, in gratitude, yielding to the Divine within us, so that it may be expressed through us, into the world around us."*

I DIDN'T KNOW I KNEW
darrell scott

When I was young and full of self,
A wise man said to me
"Someday your eyes will open, son,
Someday you'll come to see

That down beneath your ego,
Endless wisdom does abide
And all you ever need to know,
Is hidden down inside"

I thought the man was crazy,
And I laughed at what he said
He smiled and gently added,
"But it's not inside your head"

The years have flown and I have grown,
My ego left behind
A "knowing" has awakened,
From my spirit, not my mind

I'm more than just the thoughts I think,
I AM - - and that is why
In stillness I have come to know,
The Source is my supply

I understand what that old man,
Once spoke is fully true
From inward flow I've come to know,
I didn't know I knew!

Chapter 6
PROVISION
"Give us this day our daily bread"

Here for the first time is the hint of "asking". Since we are living in this physical world, even though we are not of it, we do need physical provision.

This brief request in the middle of the prayer comes with confidence, not desperate pleading. It is confident because of an awareness of the Source within.

There are two types of "bread" that we can ask for. There is the physical bread, or food, that is needed to sustain our physical bodies. But there is also the spiritual bread that is needed for our purpose and fulfillment in life. "Man shall not live by bread alone, but by every word that proceeds out of the mouth of God".

Jesus once said, "You have not because you ask not". He also said, "If we ask for bread will he give us a stone?" Why would he say that? Because sometimes when we ask for bread, He hands us what looks like a stone.

For example: Have you ever prayed for patience? If you have, you probably received a series of trials and hardships in your life. Why? Because tribulation, or hard times, produces patience. So you pray for the "bread" of patience, but you get what looks like a "stone" of tribulation. The stone is bread in disguise. The moment you bite into it, it turns into bread!

Notice that the request is not for 5 years of accumulated wealth, but simply for what is needed today - - our daily bread. Our peace and joy are not determined but how much or how little stuff we have. There are people who are worth millions that are miserable. There are people that have very little that are completely fulfilled.

Throughout history people like Buddha, Jesus, Ghandi, and Mother Teresa have shown that true wealth has nothing to do with the accumulation of stuff.

Those who have found inner peace can enjoy "stuff" without being obsessed with it. Asking for necessary provision is a legitimate part of prayer.

But in this passage of the Lord's prayer, daily bread is quite clearly not speaking of physical bread. It is speaking of spiritual bread. The Greek word used for "daily" is "espiousios" and it is the only place in the entire Bible where this particular Greek word is used.

"Espiousios" includes the word "pious", which means "sacred". It is sacred bread being spoken of here.

In James 2:15 we see a reference to "daily food". Here the word for "daily" is "ephemerou". In II Corinthans 11:28 the word "daily" is "hemeran" and is the common word for "daily", being used over 390 times in the Bible.

St. Jerome translated the Bible in the 4th century from the original Latin, Hebrew and Greek texts to form the Latin Vulgate Bible. When it came to the mysterious word "epiousios", in Matthew 6:11, he translated epiousios as "supersubstantial."

The root words are: e*pi,* meaning "above" or "super;" and *ousia,* meaning "being," "essence," or "substance." When they are read together, we come to the possible translations of "super-substantial," "above-essence," or, in effect, "supernatural" bread. This translation as supersubstantial is still found today in the Douay-Rheims Bible.

In his commentary on St. Matthew's gospel, St. Jerome states this directly: "We can also understand supersubstantial bread in another sense as bread that is above all substances and surpasses all creatures."

So this is the daily manna that sustains us one day at a time throughout our life. It is the proceeding word of God, spoken in our spirit by a still, small voice. Man shall not live by bread alone. Today if you will hear his voice. Now is the appointed time.

Hearing the voice of God within us is a skill that has to be developed. The noisy thoughts that flood our minds every day cause us to be deaf to the voice of the spirit, which is our daily bread.

There is a process which God has provided to open our ears to hear his voice. In Isaiah 50:4 it talks about God opening our ear: *" - - He wakeneth my ear to hear as the learned".*

In Job 33:14 (KJV) it says: *"God speaks once, yea twice, yet man perceiveth it not."*

God wants to 'waken our ear' but most of the time we have so much 'ear wax' in our spiritual ears that we can't hear what He's saying!" In Acts 28:27 it talks about religious people whose *"heart is waxed gross and their ears are dull of hearing"*. Our endless thoughts can create ear wax that prevents us from hearing what God is saying.

So what does it mean that *'God speaks once, yea twice'*? Well the next few verses explain the two schools of the spirit that God uses to open our ears. They are the schools of the 'still voice' and the 'steel vice'. If God can't get you to hear one way, he'll make sure you hear Him the other way!

Notice in verses 15-22 it says, *'In a dream, in a vision of the night, when deep sleep falleth upon men, in slumberings upon the bed; Then he opens the ears of men, and sealeth their instruction. That He may withdraw man from his purpose, and hide pride from man. He keepeth back his soul from the pit, and his life from perishing by the sword. He is chastened also with pain upon his bed, and the multitude of his bones with strong pain. So that his life abhorreth bread, and his soul dainty meat. His flesh is consumed away, that it cannot be seen; and his bones that were not seen stick out. Yea, his soul draweth near unto the grave, and his life to the destroyers."*

It has always been His intention to *"open our ears"* and

48

"*seal our instructions*" while we sleep. Now sleep may refer to actual nighttime slumber, but it also may be referring to resting our minds and thoughts so that we can hear. The purpose is to "*withdraw us from our own purposes*"!

However, if we are so dull of hearing that the "still voice" doesn't get through to us, the "steel vice" will. Do you know what a vice is? It's a steel contraption that you put a pipe or piece of metal in when you want to bend it. The vice is tightened and puts pressure on the pipe until it bends.

If we fail to have our ears opened by God's voice, He will allow pressure, and even pain to open them up! Remember the verse that says (Heb. 12:6-11 NIV), '*Because the Lord disciplines those He loves, and punishes everyone He accepts as a son'*. It goes on to tell us that the discipline produces a harvest of righteousness and peace.

One of my mentors, Bob Mumford used to say "God fixes a fix to fix you, if you fix your fix before you're fixed, He'll fix another fix to fix you, so brother, don't fix your fix!"

Another of his quotes was: "God has a Ways and Means Committee designing problems especially suited for your growth and development. So cultivate an attitude of gratitude in the restriction of affliction!"

So, these two "schools of the spirit" are both designed to open our ears to the voice of the spirit. The first one is to detach from our own thoughts so we can hear the still small voice. The second is far more painful. The steel vice creates enough pressure, and even pain, that forces us to hear.

Now, there's one more element to these two schools of the spirit that can help tremendously. That element is a mentor. Job 33:23 KJV says, *"If there be a messenger with him, an interpreter, one among a thousand, to show unto man His (God's) uprightness, then He is gracious unto him"*.

If you have all three of these things working together, you will learn to hear God's voice! Listening to His Word, embracing the pain of discipline, and learning from the "one in a thousand" who has already been down the path you are traveling!

Notice Job 33:29 NIV: *"God does all these things to a man – twice, even three times"*. Usually we have to be taught the same lesson more than once for it to sink in! God goes on to say in verse 33: - - *"listen to me, be silent, and I will teach you wisdom."*

As we become still and silent, he teaches us wisdom. That leads to the next step. Now we have developed a disciplined ear that allows us to acquire a disciplined tongue.

Isaiah 50:4 (KJV) says: *"The Lord God hath given me the tongue of the learned, that I should know how to speak a word in season to him that is weary - -"*

This is where the daily bread that we receive becomes a gift of life to those around us. The "tongue of the learned" gives us the wisdom to speak effectively to others.

Notice that it says, *"That I should know how"*. Because we have developed a disciplined ear, we know have the "know how" of a disciplined tongue. There are many people who have wisdom to share with others, but they lack the "know how".

The second thing is *"to speak a word"*. Too often we want to share with everyone around us everything that we know. Wisdom knows when to share and what to share with others.

The third thing is *"in season"*. We have progressed from the "know how" to the "what to speak", and now to the "when to speak it". There is a right time and a wrong time to share truth with others. Only a disciplined ear and tongue can discern how, what, and when to speak.

And finally, our tongue is disciplined to speak "to him that is weary". This is the "who do we speak to" level. We may know how to speak a word in season, but if the person we are sharing with is not weary - - if they don't yet have ears to hear - - then they may not be able to hear us at all.

Jesus understand the principle of asking for daily spiritual bread. He had a disciplined ear. He said, *"the Son can do nothing by himself; he can do only what he sees his Father doing, because whatever the Father does the Son also does".*

He also knew when to speak and when to remain silent.

DAILY BREAD
Darrell Scott

Give us our bread, that we might be fed
And may we have ears that can hear
A fresh word today, to show us the way
Destroying all worry and fear

And teach us to share, with folks everywhere
The weary and those who are broken
A word that that is real, a word that can heal
Anointing each word that is spoken

So Father, we ask, as we face the task
Of daily responding to you
For spiritual bread, that we might be fed
And lead us to feed others too

Chapter 7
PARDON
"Forgive us our trespasses, as we forgive those who trespass against us"

I have titled this chapter "Pardon" instead of "Forgiveness" simply because "pardon" begins with a "p". The chapter is really about forgiveness, however. That raises the question: What is the difference between pardon and forgiveness.

Pardon allows a person guilty of a crime to go free even though they are guilty. The victim of the one pardoned may or may not be affected, but the guilty one who is pardoned is affected greatly.

Forgiveness is just the opposite of pardon. It is primarily for the benefit of the victim, or the one who has been offended, and may, or may not affect the offender. Forgiveness does not require an acceptance on the part of the offender, and that is why it may or may not affect him or her.

Pardon is a judicial issue, while forgiveness is an issue of the heart. It is possible to pardon, but not forgive, just as it is possible to forgive without pardoning. When one who has been pardoned, not only embraces their freedom, but also embraces forgiveness from the one they victimized they are doubly free! They are free from the penalty of what they did and also free from the anger and ill-will of the one they offended.

An example of that is what happened to my daughter, Rachel, at Columbine. She was the first student to be shot and killed on April 20, 1999 by two boys armed with guns and pipe bombs.

Our family chose to forgive the teenage shooters, but we would not have pardoned them if they had lived to face criminal charges. We would have co-operated with the prosecuting attorney to ensure that they could never commit this type of heinous event again.

Forgiveness opened the door for our family to share Rachel's story over the last 2 decades to over 25,000,000 people, preventing half a dozen school shootings and saving hundreds of potential suicide victims.

While we would have supported a conviction sentence for their incarceration if they had lived - - (they committed suicide), we could not afford to live with unforgiveness in our hearts. A failure to forgive ensures that you will be victimized with anger, bitterness, and a desire for revenge, long after the initial offense is over with.

So while pardon frees the guilty one from the penalty of punishment, forgiveness frees the victim from the self-inflicted torment of anger and bitterness.

Scripture refers to both pardon and forgiveness in Micah 7:18 (NIV),

Who is a God like you, who pardons sin and forgives the transgression of the remnant of his inheritance.

In this verse we see that God not only pardons, but he also forgives. The combination of pardon and forgiveness is called "grace". He doesn't just free us from the penalty and punishment of our sin - - he also removes every trace of the transgression as though it never happened! This is pointed out by Micah in the very next verse: (Micah 7:19).

" - - you will tread our sins underfoot and hurl all our iniquities into the depths of the sea."

As spiritual beings we are having a human experience on this planet. Part of the human experience includes mistakes and wrong choices. The great 17th century writer and poet, Alexander Pope once said, *"To err is human, to forgive, divine"*. The Christian Bible says, *"Where sin abounded, grace did much more abound"*.

The ability to ask for forgiveness requires strength and humility. Acknowledging our wrongs and accepting forgiveness are part of the journey.

Un-forgiveness is a form of self-mutilation. To not forgive is to allow ourselves to be an ongoing victim. Forgiveness is not just for the one who offended, but for the person doing the forgiving. The end result of forgiveness is peace.

Peter asked Jesus, "Lord, how oft shall my brother sin against me, and I forgive him? till seven times? Jesus saith unto him, I say not unto thee, Until seven times: but, Until seventy times seven."

Obviously there is no magical number of times that you should forgive. Forgiveness is ongoing process that keeps you free.

But here is an important point. Forgiveness does not mean that you allow people to run over you or continue doing things wrong without adjustment on your part.

The same Jesus who said that we are to forgive a person 490 times in the same day, is the same Jesus who kicked over the tables of the moneychangers and drove them out of the temple!

He is the same Jesus who cursed the fig tree, and who blasted the Pharisees (religious people) for their hypocrisy.

In Matthew 5:39 Jesus said, *"But I tell you, do not resist an evil person. If anyone slaps you on the right cheek, turn to them the other cheek also."*

However, when the apostle Paul was slapped in the face, here's how he responded: *"The high priest Ananias ordered those standing near Paul to strike him on the mouth. Then Paul said to him, "God will strike you, you whitewashed wall! You sit there to judge me according to the law, yet you yourself violate the law by commanding that I be struck!"* (Acts 23:2-3 NIV)

Paul didn't turn the other cheek! He lashed out at the high priest who had ordered him to be struck.

So forgiveness is something that we are to continually do, to avoid the prison of bitterness and anger. However, how we respond to any given situation is different. It basically boils down to being led of the spirit.

Forgiveness is to be a constant attitude. However, pardon, discipline, and self defense are separate issues that may need to be addressed individually.

Once thing is clear from this portion of the Lord's prayer. Our forgiveness can be hindered when we fail to forgive others.

The following parable from Matthew 18 illustrates that well:

"Therefore, the kingdom of heaven is like a king who wanted to settle accounts with his servants. As he began the settlement, a man who owed him ten thousand bags of gold was brought to him.

Since he was not able to pay, the master ordered that he and his wife and his children and all that he had be sold to repay the debt.

At this the servant fell on his knees before him. 'Be patient with me,' he begged, 'and I will pay back everything.' The servant's master took pity on him, canceled the debt and let him go.

But when that servant went out, he found one of his fellow servants who owed him a hundred silver coins. He grabbed him and began to choke him. 'Pay back what you owe me!' he demanded.

His fellow servant fell to his knees and begged him, 'Be patient with me, and I will pay it back.'

But he refused. Instead, he went off and had the man thrown into prison until he could pay the debt. When the other servants saw what had happened, they were outraged and went and told their master everything that had happened.

Then the master called the servant in. 'You wicked servant,' he said, 'I canceled all that debt of yours because you begged me to. Shouldn't you have had mercy on your fellow servant just as I had on you?' In anger his master handed him over to the jailers to be tortured, until he should pay back all he owed.

This is how my heavenly Father will treat each of you unless you forgive your brother or sister from your heart."

Wow! That shows how important it is for us to forgive others. So many people are walking around in bondage because they fail to forgive.

That is why this the essence of the Lord's prayer is something we should address, either verbally, or quietly, in our spirit every day.

FORGIVENESS
darrell scott

Such words of wisdom I have heard
That have a deep and truthful ring
From Ghandi and Mandela too
As well as Martin Luther King
The weak cannot forgive, they said
They cling to bitterness instead

Forgiveness is misunderstood
By those who hold to pain and rage
Their freedom gone, they choose to live
Like prisoners in a dreadful cage
They can't let go, they can't forgive
And so in bondage they now live

Forgive, and you can be set free
Your life will now move on ahead
No longer bound by things long past
Existing like the walking dead
Forgiveness opens up a door
That sets you free to live, once more

Unforgiveness keeps you chained
To those who chose to do you wrong
Always seeking for revenge
Silencing your inner song
Forgive and you will find release
Into a place of perfect peace

Chapter 8
PREVENTION
"And lead us not into temptation"

As we forgive others and let go of the reins of our life, we enter into a peace that "passes understanding". It is the peace that the world (the realm of physical matter) cannot give. But it is also a peace that the world cannot take away - - unless we allow it to.

The biggest opponent to our peace, is our thought life. This is addressed throughout this book. With up to 70,000 thoughts a day rushing through our minds, we allow a veil of noise to block out the peace and stillness of God's presence within us.

One form of thought that can block our peace is temptation. All temptation, judgment, condemnation, and accusation comes from thought. So this prayer, "lead us not into temptation" may be expressed "lead us not to thoughts of temptation.

Now here is something to consider: If God *cannot* lead us into temptation why should this request be a part of this Great Prayer?

If he cannot lead us into temptation, then this part of the prayer makes no sense. So let's take a closer look at what role God plays in the temptations we face.

In the book of James it tells us that when we are tempted we should never say that we are being tempted by God, because God does not tempt anyone - - and yet in the prayer Jesus taught his disciples this phrase is included: "Lead us not into temptation".

So let's take a closer look at what James said in James 1:13-15: *"When tempted, no one should say, "God is tempting me." For God cannot be tempted by evil, nor does he tempt anyone; but each person is tempted when they are dragged away by their own evil desire and enticed. Then, after desire has conceived, it gives birth to sin; and sin, when it is full-grown, gives birth to death."*

Temptation is a lure that appeals to something in us that we desire. Remember the Tao which says, "Ever desireless one sees the mystery. Ever desiring one sees the manifestations". Temptation is the lure that awakens desire for manifestation (or material things).

So there seems to be a dichotomy here. James says, that God cannot tempt us, and Matthew and Luke wrote that we should pray that God would not lead us into temptation. So the question is: Does God play a role in our temptations? And the answer is "Yes"!

*"And it came to pass after these things, that **God did tempt Abraham**, and said unto him, Abraham: and he said, Behold, here I am. And he said, Take now thy son, thine only son Isaac, whom thou lovest, and get thee into the land of Moriah; and offer him there for a burnt offering"* Genesis 22:1-2 KJV

When Jesus was tempted by the devil in the wilderness, it was the spirit of God that led him to be tempted.

61

*"Then Jesus was **led by the Spirit** into the **wilderness to be tempted by the devil.**"* Matthew 4:1 NIV

So from the above verses we can see that God, not only allows temptation to occur, he also is instrumental in leading us into the temptation to reveal to us what is in our own heart.

In Abraham's case, the temptation was for the purpose of Abraham realizing that he would obey God at whatever cost. God already knew that Abraham would be faithful, but it was important for Abraham to know that for himself.

In Jesus's temptations, there were valid desires that were appealed to by Satan in a perverted way. He was hungry, so the temptation was to use his divine ability to turn the stones into bread.

Jesus was anointed to perform miracles and so he was tempted to demonstrate this by falling from the highest point at the top of the temple without harm.

Jesus was appointed to be the "heir of all things" and Satan appealed to this by saying, "Fall down and worship me and I will give you all the kingdoms of the world".

The point that is important to understand is that Jesus was actually tempted to do those things. The desires of hunger, anointing, and kingship were all within him.

Several years later, he was once again tempted. This time it was Judas who asked him a question about revealing himself to the world. Jesus replied, *"Hereafter I will not talk much with you: for the prince of this world cometh, and **hath nothing in me**."*

In essence Jesus was saying that Satan wanted to tempt him, but there was nothing in him that could be tempted!

In the Old Testament there is a story about King Hezekiah. God had blessed him with great wealth, but Hezekiah began to believe that it was his wisdom, not God, that was responsible for his success. So God allowed him to become very sick.

Hezekiah then repented and God restored his health. But once again, Hezekiah's pride became a problem, and once again God allowed him to become miserable. Hezekiah repented a second time around and from that point on chose to serve God. However, God wanted to reveal to Hezekiah what was in his heart, so that Hezekiah would learn to permanently trust him.

*"But when envoys were sent by the rulers of Babylon to ask him about the miraculous sign that had occurred in the land, **God left him to test him and to know everything that was in his heart**."* II Chronicles 32:31

The word test in this verse is the same Hebrew word "nasah" that was used in the verse which said, *"God did tempt Abraham."*

63

So the purpose of temptation is to reveal to us what is hidden in our heart. It appeals to the desires, whether good or bad, that are within us. A person who has no dishonesty in their heart, cannot be tempted to cheat. A person who has no desire for money, cannot be bribed. Temptation is only real if there is something within us that can be tempted.

It is important to understand that being tempted is not a sin.

"For we do not have a high priest who is unable to empathize with our weaknesses, but we have one who has been tempted in every way, just as we are--yet he did not sin." Hebrews 4:15

Jesus experience the same temptations that we face. Throughout his lifetime there were legitimate desires in him that temptation appealed to. However, he did not allow the desires to respond to the temptation.

So, to summarize: We should pray, "Father, do not allow wrong desires to be within me that will lead to temptation, and ultimately, sin". Ever desireless, one will know the mystery. Ever desiring, one will only know the manifestation.

Jesus often spoke of the "Mystery of the Kingdom". He also described it as a condition of "righteousness, peace, and joy". Many have entered the Kingdom of peace only to be lured back into the trap of egoic desires by temptation.

64

Chapter 9
PROTECTION
"but deliver us from evil"

Habakkuk 1:13 says, *"Your eyes are too pure to look on evil"*. The way God delivers us from evil, is to allow it into our lives for the purpose of maturing us to the point that we cannot even see it!

In Luke 11:34, Jesus said that if our eye is single our whole body will be full of light. What does that mean? It means that if we develop a single eye (focused eye) of faith, we can become see-throughers, not look-atters. We learn to see through every situation and circumstance and observe God at work, even if there is the appearance of evil and darkness.

Jesus said, *"But I say unto you, that ye resist not evil"*
(Matthew 5:39 KJV)

Why in the world would Jesus instruct us not to resist evil? The answer is that we empower what we resist. Evil and darkness are similar in that they both exist only as an absence of something.

Evil is the absence of good. Darkness is the absence of light. They both can be described as "voids".

The way to overcome darkness is not to curse it or worry about it or resist it. You simply bring light to the situation and - - - instantly darkness vanishes.

My poem, "Darkness Fighter" illustrates this:

65

DARKNESS FIGHTER
Darrell Scott

I cursed the darkness all night long
It wouldn't go away,
I threatened, yelled, and pleaded
But the dark was here to stay

I held an anti-darkness sign
But no one there could read it
It seemed that there was just no way
The dark could be defeated

I formed a Darkness Fighter's Club
To rid us of the plight
And many came, with hearts aflame
To purge the dark of night

We voted and we passed a bill
An anti-darkness law
We chanted at a rally
'till our vocal chords were raw

We mocked it and we called it names
We created a scandal
'till someone handed me a match
And helped me light a candle

Then suddenly the darkness fled
The room just came alive
Don't fight the night, just shine a light
And darkness can't survive!

Evil, like the darkness, is not to be resisted. It is to be replaced. Light instantly removes darkness. Good always overcomes evil.

Jesus told us not to resist evil, but then Paul gave us the formula for defeating it: *"Do not be overcome by evil, but overcome evil with good"* (Romans 12:21 NIV)

God does not remove the illusion of evil, he simply purifies us to the point that we do not fear it, because we see it for the illusion that it is. That is how he "delivers us from evil".

In Psalm 23 we are told, *"Yea, though I walk through the valley of the shadow of death, I will fear no evil. For thou art with me"*.

Evil is one of the most misunderstood things in the Bible. In our human thinking, evil is all the bad stuff that can happen to us. It brings up images of Satan, demons, lust, envy, strife, bitterness, etc.

While there is a great amount of truth to that, it is important for us to go back to the origin of evil and realize what its' purpose is. Why was evil created, and who created it?

 Must people think evil originated with the devil. Others believe that it originated when Adam and Eve disobeyed God in the Garden of Eden. However, nothing could be further from the truth. It was God himself who created evil, for a purpose.

"I form the light, and create darkness: I make peace, and create evil: I the LORD do all these things"

(Isaiah 45:7)

Some translations use the words "calamity", or "disaster", or "sorrow" instead of "evil" in an attempt to protect God's reputation. However the word, "evil" is from the Hebrew word "ra" and is the same word used for "evil" throughout the Old Testament.

In the Garden of Eden, God created the tree of the knowledge of good and evil (ra). He didn't create the tree of the knowledge of good and sorrow, or good and calamity, or good and disaster!

The verse from Isaiah also says that he created both the light and the darkness. In Genesis, it tells us that after he finished creating everything he looked at all of it and said, "It is good". So God seemed satisfied that he had done a perfect job in creating everything, including darkness and evil!

Until that issue is settled we are seeing with dual vision, not with a "single eye". Unfortunately, most religious people have a dualistic view of creation. They see two powers at work instead of just one. A dualistic view is somewhat depressing, in that there is a continual power struggle between good and evil. Between God and satan.

There is a spiritual principle that must be followed in order to see through the illusions of this world into the reality of God's purposes. That principle is to develop a 'single eye of faith'. When we see with a "single eye", the dualistic view disappears, and we only see one Source, one power, one divine plan. This is the doorway to true revelation. Jesus gave us this principle when He said:

"- - - if therefore thine *eye be single*, they whole body shall be full of light. But if thine *eye be evil*, thy whole body shall be full of darkness" (Matt. 6:22 KJV)

Normally, the opposite of 'single' is 'double', but in God's definition, the opposite of 'single' is 'evil', and results in darkness (confusion, lack of light, lack of revelation). Our vision is either 'single', resulting in light, or 'evil', resulting in darkness.

When we view God's plan with a 'single eye of faith', seeing 'Him who is Invisible' as the source of all things, we eliminate the illusion that God is fighting a losing battle for His creation. The creation was put in this condition of futility, not by its own choice (or Satan's) but by reason of Him (God) who subjected it in hope.
(Rom. 8:20)

This enables us to see that the whole creation (not part) will come into the glorious freedom of the glory of the children of God. (Rom. 8:21) As we focus on these truths with a 'single eye', the confusion of dualism disappears!

It was *God*, not Satan, who planted the tree of knowledge of good and evil in Eden. It was *God* who allowed Satan access to Adam and Eve.

69

It was *God* who withdraw His conscious presence so that Adam would be tempted and fail at his first test!

It was *God* who **"created the Waster to destroy"** (Isaiah 54:16), and it was *God* who **created evil** (Isa. 45:7 KJV) for a purpose! It was *God* who brought evil on Job for his own good (Job 42:11).

When we view all of this with 'evil' or 'dual' vision, we see two great powers struggling against each other. We, in essence, see two divinities instead of one. However, when we view things with a "single eye" we can rest in faith.

When we begin to see that Satan is merely an unwilling servant of God, who can only help fulfill the Divine Plan, things will come into focus concerning God's ultimate purposes!

Satan thought he was winning a major victory by stirring up the mob to crucify Jesus (I Cor. 2:7-8), but in doing so, he accomplished the perfect will of God, and his own ultimate defeat! So it is with all his activity; it only becomes the fertilizer for the growth of God's Kingdom.

"Why did the Gentiles rage, and peoples devise futile things? The kings of the earth took their stand, and the rulers were Gathered together against the Lord, and against His Christ. For truly in this city there were gathered together against Thy holy servant Jesus, whom Thou didst anoint, both Herod and Pontius Pilate, along

*with the Gentiles and the peoples of Israel, **to do whatever Thy hand and Thy purpose predestined to occur***". (Acts 4:26-28 NAS)

Notice that the above verse does not say "to do whatever Thy hand and Thy purpose foreknew would occur", it says, "predestined to occur"! God is always the original source because He is the one with the blueprint.

It was not the Jews, the Gentiles, or even Satan who instigated the torture and crucifixion of Jesus. It was Jehovah God Himself! This is clearly seen in a chapter from Isaiah which refers to the beating and death of Messiah:

"But the Lord (Jehovah) was pleased to crush Him, putting Him to grief" (Isa. 53:10 NAS)

The prayer "deliver us from evil" does not mean, "never allow anything bad to happen to us" or "please keep us comfortable and safe". Remember this: God will hurt you, but he will never harm you. Your comfort level is not his concern, but your maturity is!

When children are taken to the dentist or doctor by their parents, they often don't understand why their parents take them to someone who is going to hurt them, i.e. give them a shot, take a blood sample, etc.

The shot certainly hurts, but the purpose is to help the child, not harm it. The hurt is intentional to prevent greater harm.

71

This truth is not often taught in churches, that God will allow us to walk through the valley of the shadow of death for our own good.

SINGLE EYE
darrell scott

A wise old man once said to me
"Don't trust the things your eyes can see
For if you do, you'll know confusion
Always judging by illusion

Don't look at - - see through my friend
Beyond the frown, the sneer, the grin
Peer deep into the living soul
Where beauty, wonders will unfold

Fear and judgment fall apart
When your view is from the heart
So don't look at, adjust your view
And focus deeper, seeing through

Deliver us from all the fear
Of evil, that can seem so near
Developing a single eye
That sees right through the devil's lie

Chapter 10
POSSESSION
"For thine is the kingdom"

The Lord's prayer begins with the prominence of the Father as the Source of all things. It ends with the acknowledgment that the kingdom, and the power, and the glory, are all his.

Let's break this down into three parts: #1 The Kingdom, #2 The Power, and #3 The Glory.

Today in religious circles the word "church" is used much more than the word "kingdom". We hear phrases such as, "Which church do you belong to?" or "It's time to go to church" or "Our church is having a banquet next Friday night".

These phrases would have sounded very strange to people in the days of Jesus. The word "church" did not exist.

In many translations of the Bible, the word "church" is used, but it should have been the word "assembly". Quite a few Bible translations use the word "congregation" or "assembly" instead of "church". The Greek word that it is translated from is "ekklesia".

Ekklesia is made up of two separate Greek words. The first is "ek" which means "out from and to". The second is "kaleo" which means "call". So, the word "ekklesia" means "the ones called out from something to something".

Peter would describe the ekklesia this way: *"But ye are a chosen generation, a royal priesthood, an holy nation, a peculiar people; that ye should shew forth the praises of him who hath called you out of darkness into his marvellous light"* (I Peter 2:9 KJV)

Notice Peter said he called us OUT of darkness INTO light. This is "ekklesia", "called out from and to".

Jesus only mentioned the word 3 times. And when he used the word "ekklesia", which unfortunately was translated "church", it had nothing to do with a building, denomination, or physical location. It strictly referred to the people who gathered in his name.

Let's take a look at the origin of the word "church". It did not come from the Greek language at all. It came from Old English and German word "kirche", which means "pertaining to the Lord".

It's equivalent in Greek is the words "kuriakos" and appears only twice in the New Testament. It is in I Corinthians 11:20 where it refers to the Lord's supper. It is also in Revelation 1:19 where it refers to the Lord's day.

So the New Testament ekklesia was any gathering of 2 or more believers, representing the Kingdom of God, not the kingdom of Rome.

Jesus said, *"For where two or three gather in my name, there am I with them."*

74

But while Jesus only uses the word "ekklesia" 3 times, he uses the word "kingdom" 127 times!

Jesus's message was that the ekklesia, or the assembly, were "called out" to proclaim the kingdom of God. The ekklesia are the messengers, while the kingdom is the message.

"For thine is the kingdom" is a phrase pregnant with meaning. Jesus said, *"Fear not, little flock; for it is your Father's good pleasure to give you the kingdom."*
(Luke 12:32 KJV)

This is an amazing gift - - a divine possession! It is his good pleasure to give us his kingdom. And, as we have already seen, the kingdom is within us. It is the prized possessions of peace and joy that are manifested as we come into alignment (righteousness) with his will.

But that kingdom which is within us is so powerful that eventually it will cause every kingdom to become a part of God's kingdom.

"The kingdoms of the world did become those of our Lord and of His Christ, and he shall reign to the ages of the ages." (Revelation 11:15 Young's Literal Translation)

In Daniel chapter 2, Daniel interprets a vision that was given to King Nebuchadnezzar of Babylon. In the vision, the king saw a stone cut out of a mountain by God's hand that smashed all the kingdoms of this world.

The stone grew until it became a great mountain that filled the whole earth.

This was a prophesy that is fulfilled in Revelation 11:15, where the kingdoms of this world become the kingdom of our Lord and of His Christ.

"He made known to us the mystery of his will according to his good pleasure, which he purposed in Christ, to be put into effect when the times reach their fulfillment—to bring unity to all things in heaven and on earth under Christ." (Ephesians 1:9-10 NIV)

In the verses you just read from Ephesians, God reveals to us the mystery of his kingdom, which is to bring unity to all things. This will happen when "the times reach their fulfillment.

What a glorious mission has been give to us, the ekklesia! It is to participate in the mystery of the kingdom which will result in the kingdom of God filling the earth, overtaking every human kingdom.

This is a little bigger vision than just getting people to attend a church service on Sunday.

This vision of the kingdom growing until it fills everything is seen again in Colossians 1:18-20:

"And he is the head of the body, the church; he is the beginning and the firstborn from among the dead, so that in everything he might have the supremacy. For God was pleased to have all his fullness dwell in him,

and through him to reconcile to himself all things,
whether things on earth or things in heaven, by making
peace through his blood, shed on the cross."

Reread those verses about 5 times, or until it sinks in
that what he is saying is that *EVERYTHING* will be
reconciled to him! What a magnificent goal!

The prophet Isaiah saw that his government, his
kingdom would continue to expand:

"Of the increase of his government and peace there
shall be no end." (Isaiah 9:7 KJV)

When we look at the world today, it seems impossible
that the worlds' governments could ever come together.
We see the clash between dictatorships, socialism,
democracy, and communism. We see the endless wars
and conflicts, and through human eyes, there appears no
way for true unity and harmony to ever happen.

But when we view things through the eyes of the spirit,
with single vision, we can be confident that God's
kingdom will prevail over all.

The kingdom belongs to him - - for *"thine is the*
kingdom"! And he that has begun a good work, will
complete it.

TWO VIEWPOINTS
Darrell Scott

Through ages past the scene unfolds,
spread out for all to see
For most it seems a conflict
sparked by a mutiny

Satan, that old serpent
Leads forth a mighty clan
A third of all the angels
To destroy Jehovah's plan

Then slipping through the Garden
The Deceiver gives his call
And tragically the two respond
Resulting in a fall

From tempter Satan has evolved
Into the great Accuser
And up to now it would appear
That God has been the loser!

But when observed with 'single eye'
This battle of confusion
Is not a conflict after all
It's only an illusion

There is no struggle on God's part
For He is in control
He has created evil for a purpose – we are told

And who subjected all of us
To such a vain condition?
Romans 8 verse 20 says
It wasn't our volition

But He who purposed everything
Is fully in command
And all of His creation shall
Fulfill the Sovereign's plan

Yes, every knee shall bow
And every tongue confess His name
And every living creature will
His Majesty proclaim

Then strife shall cease, and wickedness
Oppression, and discord
As kingdoms of this world become
THE KINGDOM OF OUR LORD!

Satan's plan will fall apart
His captives will go free
As He who owns the key to death
Proclaims their liberty

The whole creation's in travail
Just listen to its call
To be brought forth in victory
WHEN GOD IS ALL IN ALL!

Chapter 11
POWER
" - - and the power"

The end of the Lord's prayer says, "For thine is the kingdom, and the power, and the glory". We have looked at the first part of this trilogy - - the kingdom.

Now let's take a look at the "power" part. Jesus promised us that we would receive power after his Holy Spirit came to us.

"But you will receive power when the Holy Spirit comes on you; and you will be my witnesses in Jerusalem, and in all Judea and Samaria, and to the ends of the earth"
(Acts 1:8 NIV)

Jesus spoke about religious people who talk up a good game, but have no power. He described them as *"having a form of godliness, but denying the power thereof."* (II Timothy 2:5 KJV)

He also said, *"For the kingdom of God [is] not in word, but in power."* (I Corinthians 4:20)

The secret to experience the kingdom of peace and joy within us, is to still our thoughts and tune in to the still small voice of the spirit within. It is also the secret to engaging the power that God had given us.

I can tell you that in my own life, I labored and strived to do God's will. I memorized hundreds of scripture verses, prayed an hour a day, and fasted one day a

80

week. But all that activity produced very little results. I was secretly frustrated and unfulfilled. I had not yet experienced a "separation of soul and spirit". I was trying to serve God in my own strength.

When I learned the secret of quieting my mind and entering stillness, everything changed. As I obeyed the verse to *"be still and know that I am God"*, I began to find purpose, direction, and the power to fulfill what I felt in my spirit I was to do.

As I look back over the past few years, I am amazed at how God has allowed me to be an influence in the lives of millions of people around the globe. I feel very humbled to look back and see that I have met with 3 Presidents of the United States, spoken before Congress, published 12 books, spoken to over 5 million people in live settings, appeared on numerous national television shows, and been on the cover of Time magazine.

But I can not brag about any of that or take credit. First of all, it all happened through my weakness, not my strength. The death of my precious daughter, Rachel, was part of the reason all of that happened.

Another thing I am amazed about is what I have experienced in Mexico with my close friend, Dr. Mark Hanby. I have witnessed around 5,000 people have a spiritual awakening, as well as our program, Rachel's Challenge reaching many students in the schools there.

We have witnessed the power of God's kingdom in the lives of so many people there, including transformation in the lives of former hitmen for notorious drug lords.

So, when I write about the power of God, it is not theory for me. I have seen it firsthand, over and over again.

So, how can you live and walk in the power that I am writing about. First of all, understand that the Father's desire to give you the kingdom. Understand that he has promised you his power through his spirit.

But the only way to access that power is through surrender, weakness, and stillness.

"Yet those who wait for the LORD Will gain new strength; They will mount up with wings like eagles, They will run and not get tired, They will walk and not become weary." (Isaiah 40:31 NAS)

Paul was a man who experienced the power of God in a tremendous way. He was used to heal the sick, cast out demons, break out of prisons, and impact thousands of lives. He gave us his secret:

"And he said unto me, My grace is sufficient for thee: for my strength is made perfect in weakness. Most gladly therefore will I rather glory in my infirmities, that the power of Christ may rest upon me."
(II Corinthians 12:9 KJV)

We saw in the previous chapter that his kingdom will continue to grow until the kingdoms of this world become the kingdoms of our Lord and his Christ.

Since he is *"upholding all things by the word of his power"* (Hebrews 1:3 KJV), he certainly has the ability to reconcile everything unto himself.

It is interesting to note that quantum physics now is telling us that the whole universe is held together by vibrating strings of energy. They call it "string theory". They describe exactly what Hebrews 1:3 says. It is the "word of his power" is holding everything together!

The following scriptures tell us that every power, ruler, and authority were created by him and for him. It ends with the declaration that all things will be reconciled through the sacrifice of his blood, shed on the cross.

"For by him all things were created: things in heaven and on earth, visible and invisible, whether thrones or powers or rulers or authorities; all things were created by him and for him. He is before all things, and in him all things hold together. And he is the head of the body, the church; he is the beginning and the firstborn from among the dead, so that in everything he might have the supremacy. For God was pleased to have all his fullness dwell in him, and through him to reconcile to himself all things, whether things on earth or things in heaven, by making peace through his blood, shed on the cross."
(Colossians 1:15–20)

PEACE and POWER
Darrell Scott

Oh mighty sage, great man of peace
Such wisdom you have spoken
How can my inner turmoil cease?
He said, "You must be broken"

Your gifts and talents, waste away
Where ego does abound
Humility must rule the day
Or peace will not be found

Resist and you will only know
Anxiety and pain
But let your inner being flow
And peace will always reign

Embrace the pace, and yield to grace
Just let your mind be stilled
With dignity, you'll find your place
And live a life fulfilled

Your power and your strength will flow
Within a quieted mind
In stillness you will come to know
His power, so divine

Chapter 12
PRESENCE
"and the glory"

We have seen that the "ekklesia" is the "called out ones" who are commissioned to proclaim, and bring the kingdom of God to the whole world.

The gospel (which means "good news") begins with the message of reconciliation. The following verses show the purpose and mission of the ekklesia:

"For Christ's love compels us, because we are convinced that one died for all, and therefore all died. And he died for all, that those who live should no longer live for themselves but for him who died for them and was raised again. So from now on we regard no one from a worldly point of view. Though we once regarded Christ in this way, we do so no longer. Therefore, if anyone is in Christ, the new creation has come: The old has gone, the new is here! All this is from God, who reconciled us to himself through Christ and gave us the ministry of reconciliation: that God was reconciling the world to himself in Christ, not counting people's sins against them. And he has committed to us the message of reconciliation. We are therefore Christ's ambassadors, as though God were making his appeal through us. We implore you on Christ's behalf: Be reconciled to God."

(II Corinthians 5:14-20 NIV)

Several very important things are said in the above verses that you seldom, or never, hear in church sermons.

#1 Christ died for ALL - - therefore ALL died!
This is reflected in I Corinthians 15:22, *"For as in Adam all die, even so in Christ shall all be made alive. But every man in his own order"*

#2 Christ reconciled us and gave us the ministry of reconciliation. Here is the purpose for which the ekklesia was called. To proclaim to the world that they have already been reconciled to God!

#3 In reconciling the world though Christ, God no longer counts peoples sins against them!

The good news (Gospel) is that *"The Lord is not slack concerning his promise, as some men count slackness; but is longsuffering to us-ward, not willing that any should perish, but that all should come to repentance."*
(II Peter 3:9 KJV)

The word "willing" used in this verse is the Greek word "boulomai" which means "intent" or "purpose".

There are two basic Greek words for the "will" of God. These words are "thelema" and "boulema". "Thelema", according to W.E.Vine's Dictionary of N.T. Words, means: "God's gracious design".

Some say that it indicates "desire" rather than "purpose". "Thelema" also had connecting words, such as, "thelesis" and "thelo".

The second Greek word for the "will" of God is "boulema" and, according to Vine's, means "a deliberate design, that which is purposed". It is agreed that this word is used for the 'predetermined counsels of God that cannot be changed"! "Boulema" is also connected to the word "boulomai".

Look at I Timothy 2:4 to illustrate the use of the Greek word "thelo" concerning God's view of the eternal destiny of mankind. KJV reads, "Who *will* have all men to be saved". The word "will" is from "thelo". NAS reads, "Who **desires** all men to be saved".

The KJV certainly uses stronger language than the NAS. However, since the Greek word "thelo" is used here, it does seem to be expressing the desire of God that all would be saved.

I don't think anyone would argue against the belief that God desires everyone to be saved. Now let's take a look at the "predetermined counsel and purpose" of God. In the middle of describing the judgments of God, Peter reminds us of God's ultimate purpose is that none would perish and that all would repent. Reread II Peter 3:9.

Here, the word translated "willing" is from the Greek word "boulomai", portraying the 'predetermined purpose' of God! He literally has not *purposed* that any should perish! This same word "boulomai" is used in Acts 5:28 as "intend" and in Acts 12:4 as "intending".

It is used in James 1:18 where it says: "In the exercise of His *will* (boulomai) He brought us forth by the word of truth". It was not the exercise of His "wish", but of His "purpose".

The NAS waters the word "boulomai" in II Pet. 3:9 down to the word "wishing", which is a perversion of scholastic integrity in translation.

So we see that both God's desire (thelo) and His purpose (boulomai) is that **ALL** should come to repentance and be saved!

What did Peter mean when he said, "the Lord is not slack concerning His promise"? Could he be referring to the promise from Isaiah 45:22-24 where He swore that all of mankind would indeed turn to Him and be saved? I think so!

Also, note that the Lord is "longsuffering - - - not willing (boulomai) that any should perish". Peter then says to "account that the longsuffering of our Lord is salvation" (II Pet. 3:15).

It was obvious from the Old Testament that God intended to fulfill **ALL** of His "good pleasure" (thelema) and his "purpose" (boulema). How can you read Isaiah 46:10 and come to any other conclusion?

So what does all of this have to do with the "glory" of God mentioned at the end of the Lord's prayer?

It has to do with his ultimate purpose, and that purpose is to fill the whole earth with his glory as the kingdoms of this world become the kingdom of our Lord and his Christ.

"For the earth will be filled with the knowledge of the glory of the LORD as the waters cover the sea."
(Habakkuk 2:14 NIV)
"But as truly as I live, all the earth shall be filled with the glory of the LORD." (Numbers 14:21 KJV)

How is the glory of the Lord going to fill the earth? It will happen through the ekklesia.

"Arise, shine, for your light has come, and the glory of the Lord rises upon you. See, darkness covers the earth and thick darkness is over the peoples, but the Lord rises upon you and his glory appears over you. Nations will come to your light, and kings to the brightness of your dawn." (Isaiah 60:1-3 NIV)

All of these scriptures point to a time when everything will be reconciled back to God.

"Therefore God exalted him to the highest place and gave him the name that is above every name that at the name of Jesus every knee should bow, in heaven and on earth and under the earth, and every tongue acknowledge that Jesus Christ is Lord, to the glory of God the Father." (Philippians 2:9-11 NIV)

We have heard this verse quoted many times, but have

89

we ever really considered the amazing truth that it contains?

It says that EVERY KNEE shall bow and EVERY TONGUE shall acknowledge that Jesus is Lord! And it is to the glory of God the Father! God does not receive glory from forced submission. There is no hint of forced submission in these verses.

In fact, these verses originated in the book of Isaiah in the Old Testament:

"And there is no God apart from me, a righteous God and a Savior; there is none but me. "Turn to me and be saved, all you ends of the earth; for I am God, and there is no other. By myself I have sworn, my mouth has uttered in all integrity a word that will not be revoked: Before me every knee will bow; by me every tongue will swear. They will say of me, 'In the LORD alone are deliverance and strength." (Isaiah 45:21-24 NIV)

It could not be any plainer! God has sworn and his word will not be revoked that every knew will bow and every tongue swear that in the Lord alone is deliverance and strength!

So - - the kingdom is his, and it will overcome every other kingdom. They will all become a part of his kingdom. The power is his, and it will accomplish his purpose. And finally, the glory is his - - the glory that will fill the earth and reconcile everything in heaven and in earth to him!

Chapter 13
PERMANENCE in PERSPECTIVE
"forever, amen"

This chapter will be the most controversial chapter in this book. Buckle your seat belt and follow closely, read carefully, and remain open to fresh understanding!

Have I got your attention? I hope so. Because I am about to make 3 radical statements that will be backed up by original scripture.

Here we go:
#1 The word "forever" in this verse is not accurate.
#2 Christ's kingdom will come to an end
#3 Jesus is not the Eternal King

Now, before you burn this book - - please take the time to read and challenge this entire chapter.

You will discover that:
#1 The word "forever" should be "ages"
#2 Christ's kingdom lasts for the ages, but does end
#3 Jesus is the King of the Ages, not the Eternal King

You will also discover why this is important and how it can change your perspective concerning God's purposes for you and for the whole creation.

I began this book by discussing the importance of "awareness" meditation as a prelude to prayer. It is so important to disengage from our thought life and enter into the stillness of the spirit, where true prayer can emerge.

The Lord's prayer gives us the pattern that will enable us to *pray without ceasing* as Paul so aptly put it in I Thessalonians 5:13.

As we have thoroughly examined the prayer given by Jesus to his disciples we have seen that it was never intended to be a memorized chant, but a pattern of prayer to live by. We have examined the following pattern:

Prominence: "Our Father"
Place: "Which art in heaven"
Praise: "Hallowed be thy name"
Participation: "Thy kingdom come. Thy will be done on earth, as it is in heaven."
Provision: "Give us this day our daily bread"
Pardon: "And forgive us our debts, as we forgive our debtors"
Prevention: "And lead us not into temptation"
Protection: "But deliver us from evil"
Possession: "For thine is the kingdom - -
Power: "- - and the power - -
Presence: "- - and the glory"
Permanence in Perspective: "Forever. Amen"

Now we come to the last two words - - "forever" and "amen". Both seem to denote finality - - permanence. However, the word "forever" comes from the Greek word, "aionas" and literally means "ages".

The word is 'aionios' and is an adjective of the noun 'aion' which means 'age'. 'Aion' is where we get the word 'eon' or 'age'. 'Aionios' should always be translated 'age-abiding' or 'age-lasting' or 'of the ages'. It should *NEVER* have been translated 'forever' or 'eternal'!

The words 'aion' and 'aionios' occur 199 times in the New Testament. They are translated as follows in the King James Version:

"AION"				"AIONIOS"	
AGES	2	NEVER	7	EVERLASTING	25
COURSE	1	EVERMORE	4	ETERNAL	42
WORLD	40	ETERNAL	2	WORLD	3
EVER	72			EVER	1

This is unbelievable! For a translator to translate the exact same Greek word into 7 different English words that completely contradict each other is insanity! The same word 'aion' is said to mean 'never' in one place and 'evermore' in another.

One time it is translated 'world' and a few verses later the same identical word is translated 'eternal' or 'course'! To see this kind of "butchering" in translation going on is outrageous! Thank God, there were a few translators who were consistent with their translation of these words.

When these words are accurately and consistently translated, we see a pattern of "sound words" emerge. For example, let's look at I Timothy 1:17 NAS:

"Now unto the **KING ETERNAL, IMMORTAL**, invisible, the only God be honor and glory forever and ever. Amen."

Now let's view the exact same verse from Rotherham's and Young's translations:

"and to the **KING OF THE AGES, THE INCORRUPTIBLE**, invisible, only wise God, is honor and glory – to the ages of the ages! Amen."

How often have we heard Jesus referred to as the Eternal King - - when in original scripture he is not called that. He is called the King of the Ages.

The reason he is called the King of the Ages, is because his kingdom will come to an end. Don't believe me - - believe the scriptures:

"Then the end will come, when he hands over the kingdom to God the Father after he has destroyed all dominion, authority and power. For he must reign until he has put all his enemies under his feet. The last enemy to be destroyed is death. For he "has put everything under his feet." Now when it says that "everything" has been put under him, it is clear that this does not include God himself, who put everything under Christ. When he has done this, then the Son

94

himself will be made subject to him who put everything under him, so that God may be all in all."

(I Corinthians 15:24-28 NIV)

These previous verses contain some amazing declarations! First, it is the only place in the Bible that tells us what happens at the end of the ages - - *"then end will come"*. What happens? *"He* (Jesus) *hands over the kingdom to God the Father"*! Notice a few words later where it says, *"For he must reign until"*.

If I said to you, I am going to sit here until - - , it indicates that I will sit here until a certain thing happens, and then I will no longer sit here. For Christ to reign until, indicates that the reign will end when the "until" happens.

In these verses it tells us what the "until" means. It means until everything has been made subject to God through Christ. All enemies have been destroyed, including death. This would include the lake of fire which is called the "second death" (Revelation 20:14).

Once that is accomplished, the kingdom reign that has lasted throughout the ages comes to an end, and the King, the son himself, is subject to the Father, that God may be all in all! This is the view we are given from the Bible. In the beginning - - God - - in the end - - God.

The difference in translation is radical! Now, let's look at another verse that really shows us the problem with KJV's translation of the word 'aion'.

*"- - but whosoever speaketh against the Holy Ghost, it shall not be forgiven him, **neither in this world, neither in the world to come**."* (Matthew 12:32 KJV)

Even the New American Standard differs with the KJV in this verse:

"- - but whosoever shall speak against the Holy Spirit, it shall not be forgiven him, *either in this age, or in the age to come*." (Matthew 12:32 NAS)

Since there are "ages yet to come" (Eph. 2:7), it is easy to see that while a person committing the sin of speaking against the Holy Spirit may not be forgiven in the age Jesus spoke of, or the age following, this does not create a permanently "unpardonable sin", as many would want us to believe.

Truth should be allowed to stand on its own merits. It should not be at the mercy of translators who do not want to risk "upsetting the applecart" of current theology. Incidentally, some translators were instructed (such as the King James translators) not to alter current theology in their translating by political or theological authorities of their day.

We forget that the King James who ordered the KJV to be translated was the same King James that fled to America as Pilgrims because of the persecution they received at his hand. Here is another example of gross mistranslation of the word 'aion'.

"Who hath saved us, and called us with an holy calling, not according to our works, but according to His own purpose and grace, which was given us in Christ Jesus *before the world began*" (II Tim. 1:9 KJV)

The KJV translators take the word 'aion' and translate it into the word 'world' here. They do not translate it 'ever', 'never', or 'eternal' because these words would make no sense in this verse. Phrases like 'before the never began' or 'before the never began' or 'before the eternal began' would make absolutely no sense!

Instead, they chose to insert the word 'world' in this verse! Why didn't they simply translate it 'age' which is the only accurate translation of the word 'aion'?

The word for 'world' comes from the Greek words 'kosmos', from which we derive 'cosmos' or 'world'. If 'world' were the right word to be translated here, the Greek word would have been 'kosmos', not 'aion'.

Rotherham's and Young's translate this 'before the age-times' which is correct. Even the NAS uses the correct wording here as 'age'.

Paul instructed us to "*Hold fast the form of sound words*" (II Timothy 1:13 KJV). As you can see there is a big difference between "forever" and "age" or between "world" and "never". And yet all of these words come from the exact same word in Greek: "aion" which should always be translated "age".

97

So, at the end of the Lord's prayer, the real wording should be: "For thine is the kingdom, and the power, and the glory, throughout the ages. Amen."

WE HAVE BEEN BLINDED TO THE TRUE PURPOSES OF GOD THROUGH THE MISTRANSLATION OF SUCH WORDS AS 'AION' AND 'AINIOS'! IT HIDES THE FACT THAT GOD HAS A 'PURPOSE OF THE AGES' EPH. 3:11, HE IS THE 'KING OF THE AGES' I TIM. 1:17, HE APPOINTED JESUS AS THE 'HEIR OF ALL THINGS' THROUGH WHOM HE 'MADE THE AGES' HEB. 1:2 AND 'PREPARED THE AGES' BY HIS WORD HEB. 11:3. HE HAS GIVE TO US 'LIFE OF THE AGES' JOHN 3:16 AND HAS APPOINTED A 'JUDGMENT OF THE AGES' HEB. 6:2 FOR THE UNREPENTENT, EVEN FOR THOSE WHO SHALL NOT RECEIVE FORGIVENESS IN 'THIS AGE', OR THE 'AGE TO COME' MATT. 12:32

The permanence at the end of the Lord's prayer is real. His kingdom will come and his will be done on earth as it is in heaven. The kingdoms of this world will become the kingdoms of the Lord and his Christ.

And then the permanence of the ages will become the permanence of the eternal as God becomes "all in all"!

OTHER BOOKS BY DARRELL SCOTT
Go to www.dscottbooks.com or
Go to Amazon and type in "books by Darrell Scott"

Darrell Scott has authored, or co-authored several published books, including the best-seller,

Rachel's Tears, the story of his daughter, Rachel, the first victim of the Columbine high school shootings.

Darrell and his wife Sandy started a non-profit organization called, *Rachel's Challenge*, in Rachel's memory. Through its 40 presenters, Rachel's Challenge has reached over 28 million people in live settings over the last 18 years.

Rachel's Challenge has won 3 Emmy Awards through its television partners. They partner with Chuck and Gena Norris by providing character programming for the Norris's "KickStart Kids" organization. They also partner with the Cal Ripken, Sr. Foundation as well as with Marzano Research, one of the most prestigious K-12 research firms in the nation.

Darrell has appeared on numerous television programs such as Oprah, Larry King Live, Good Morning America, Dateline, O'Reilly Factor, Anderson Cooper, etc. He has been featured on the cover of Time magazine and quoted in Newsweek, the Wall Street Journal, and many other publications.

Darrell does keynote addresses for leadership teams of such organizations as Southwest Airlines, Bank of America, Sprint, BNSF Railroad, Motorola, and many others. He has met with Presidents Clinton, Bush, and Trump several times.

Darrell and his wife, Sandy, live in Lone Tree, Colorado where they enjoy their children and grandchildren.

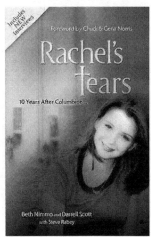

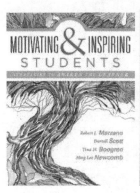

OTHER BOOKS BY DARRELL SCOTT

Made in the USA
San Bernardino, CA
12 January 2019